Princess Claire

and the Curious Cousins

A Christmas Story

Carol Caldwell

BLUE FORGE PRESS
Port Orchard, Washington

Princess Claire and the Curious Cousins: A Christmas Story
Copyright 2023
by Carol Caldwell

First eBook Edition October 2023
First Print Edition October 2023

ISBN 978-1-59092-914-8

All rights reserved, including the right to reproduce this book or portions thereof in any form whatsoever, except in the case of short excerpts for use in reviews of the book.

For information about film, reprint or other subsidiary rights, contact blueforgegroup@gmail.com

This is a work of fiction. Names, characters, locations, and all other story elements are the product of the authors' imaginations and are used fictitiously. Any resemblance to actual persons, living or dead, or other real life situations is purely coincidental.

Blue Forge Press is the print division of the volunteer-run, federal 501(c)3 nonprofit company, Blue Forge Group, founded in 1989 and dedicated to bringing light to the shadows and voice to the silence. We strive to empower storytellers across all walks of life with our four divisions: Blue Forge Press, Blue Forge Films, Blue Forge Gaming, and Blue Forge Records. Find out more at www.BlueForgeGroup.org

Blue Forge Press
7419 Ebbert Drive Southeast
Port Orchard, Washington 98367
blueforgepress@gmail.com
360-550-2071 ph.txt

This book is dedicated to my granddaughter Claire, who got me started writing and is the inspiration for the Princess Claire series.

Princess Claire
and the Curious Cousins

Carol Caldwell

Chapter One

Princess Claire stared at the huge tree standing in the middle of the main hall. It reached all the way to the balcony on the second floor. Around the tree were boxes of red, green, gold, and silver ornaments, too many to count. Claire saw her mother watching her. She ran over to the Queen and gave her a big hug. "It will be so beautiful when it's decorated. I love Christmas." Claire said. "Can I help trim the tree?"

"Of course, you can, but only as high as you can reach. Jiggles will use the ladder to go to the top."

Her mother paused with her finger resting on her chin. "Did I tell you that your cousins Ella and Grissella are coming to visit us?"

"No," Claire sighed. Her shoulders slumped. Her cousins were near Claire's age and they loved visiting the Castle. But they had so much energy that Claire couldn't keep up with them.

She asked, "When?"

Her mother told her "In three days."

Claire thought, *I better start planning things to keep them busy.*

Chapter Two

Snow fell on the cousins' arrival day. Flakes splashed in large puddles that froze over. The girls rushed out of their carriage into the castle hall to avoid getting wet.

Claire was there to meet them. The girls were twins, but they didn't dress alike. Ella chose mostly blue dresses to go with her bright blond hair, but Grissella picked green dresses to set off her *very* blond hair. Claire hoped they never changed their colors, or she wouldn't be able to tell who was who. The twins squealed over the beautiful

Christmas tree in the center of the hall.

Before Claire could even say hello, they began fingering the ornaments, moving them from one branch to another.

Ella said, "Why aren't there any blue ones?"

Then Grissella stuck her nose in the air and said, "It's because blue isn't

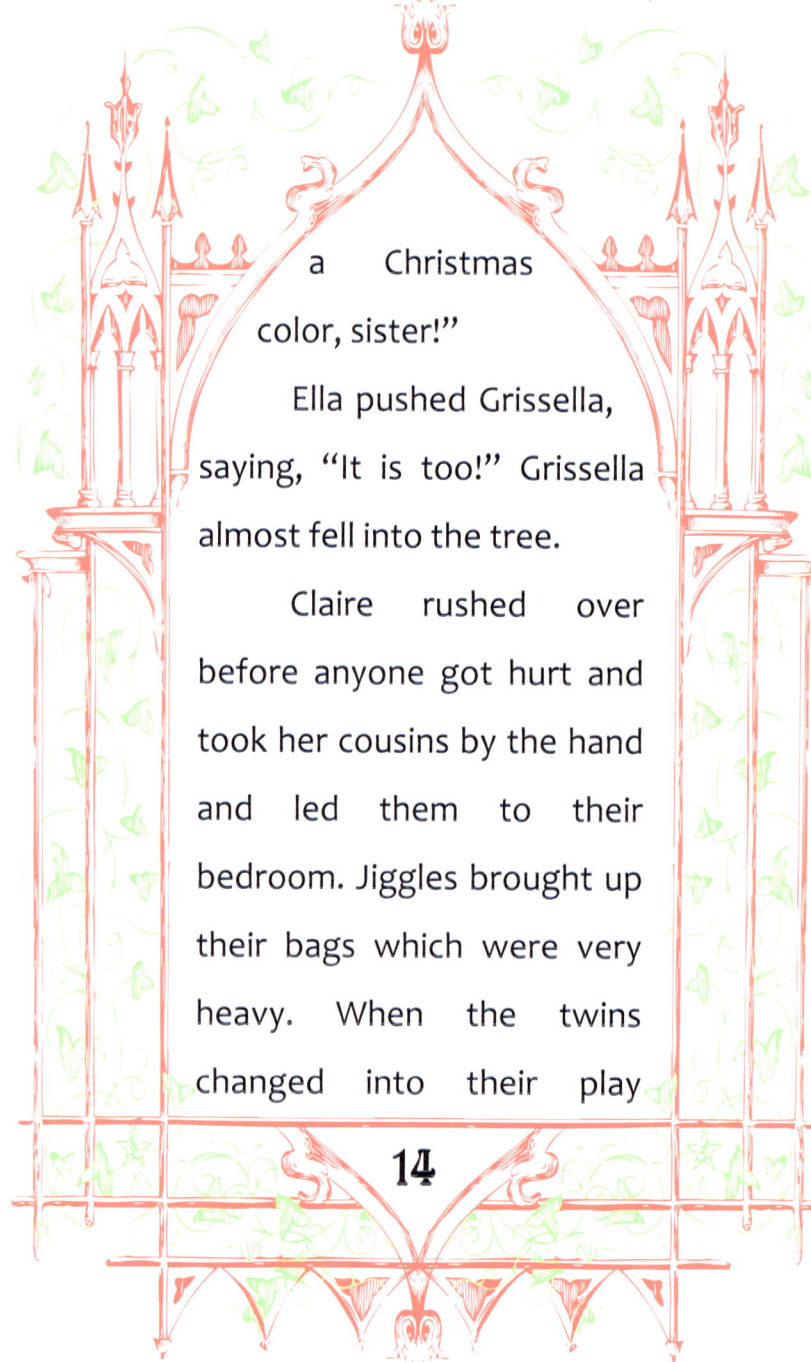

a Christmas color, sister!"

Ella pushed Grissella, saying, "It is too!" Grissella almost fell into the tree.

Claire rushed over before anyone got hurt and took her cousins by the hand and led them to their bedroom. Jiggles brought up their bags which were very heavy. When the twins changed into their play clothes, Claire took them into the Playroom. She had asked her mother to have three small trees set up on stands for them to decorate.

Claire explained to her cousins that they would string cranberries and popcorn to make garlands to decorate the trees with. Claire showed them how to do it.

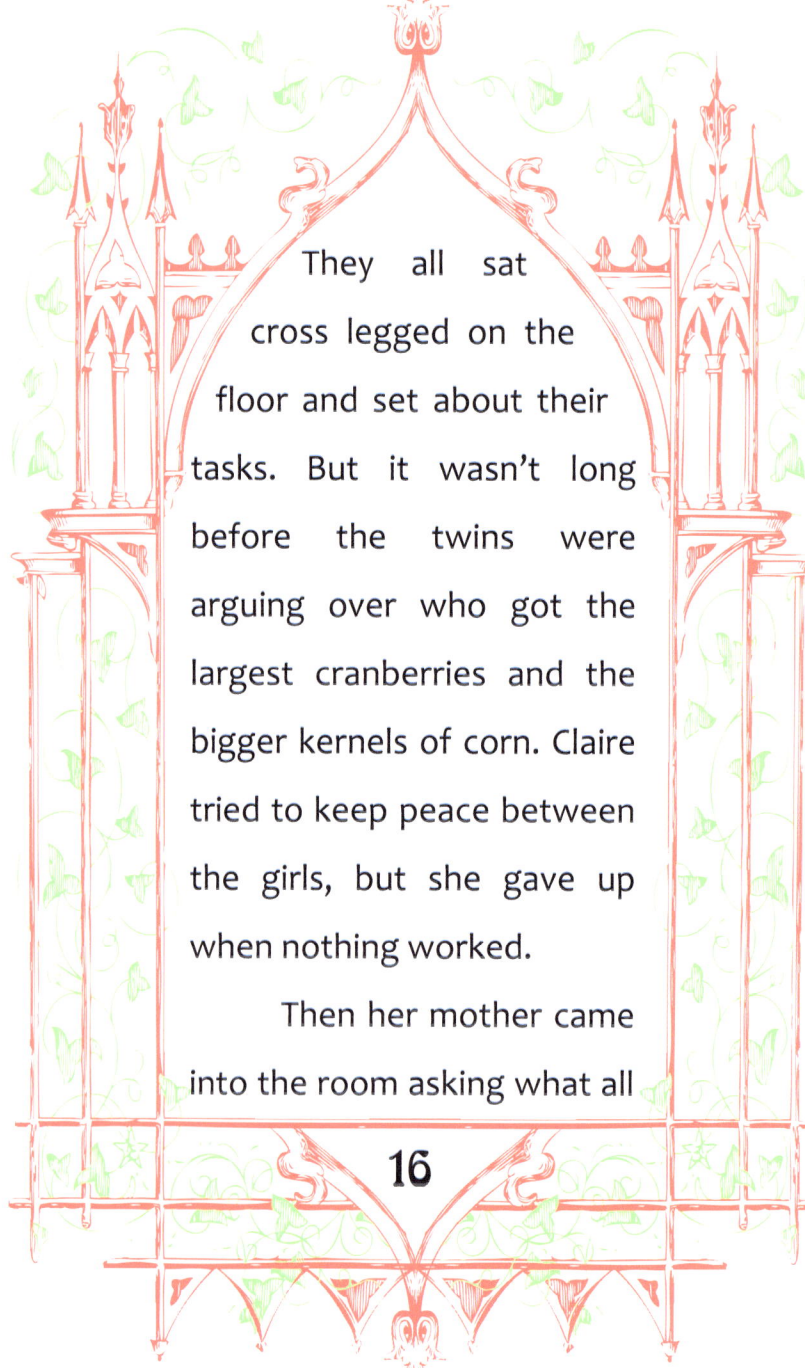

They all sat cross legged on the floor and set about their tasks. But it wasn't long before the twins were arguing over who got the largest cranberries and the bigger kernels of corn. Claire tried to keep peace between the girls, but she gave up when nothing worked.

Then her mother came into the room asking what all

the fuss was about. "I can hear your shouts and shrieks as far away as the kitchen. Claire, can you keep the noise down, please?"

Claire nodded her head and said, "Yes, ma'am." After her mother left, Claire whispered to her cousins, "Don't argue so much. You are ladies and ladies don't shout in the castle. Only outside."

Claire smiled. She thought her cousins might like to know an alternative to being quiet because they were not usually quiet girls.

With the trees decorated, Claire took her cousins outside to play in the snow. Naturally the twins' snow outfits were color-coordinated with Ella in blue

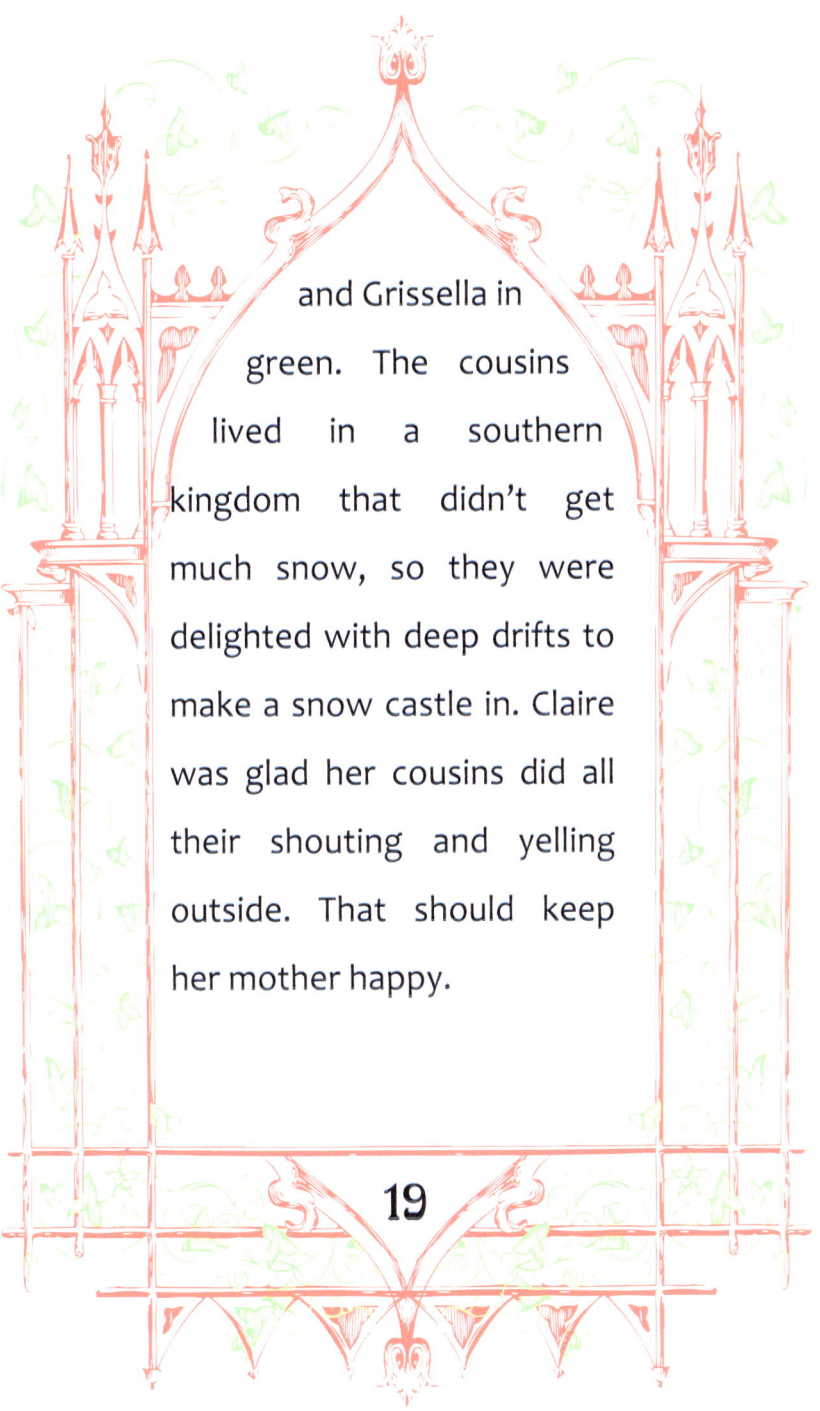

and Grissella in green. The cousins lived in a southern kingdom that didn't get much snow, so they were delighted with deep drifts to make a snow castle in. Claire was glad her cousins did all their shouting and yelling outside. That should keep her mother happy.

Chapter Three

The next morning when Claire came down for breakfast, she found the twins in the main hall scrambling through wrapped packages under the tree. She put her hands on the sides of her face and moaned. Then

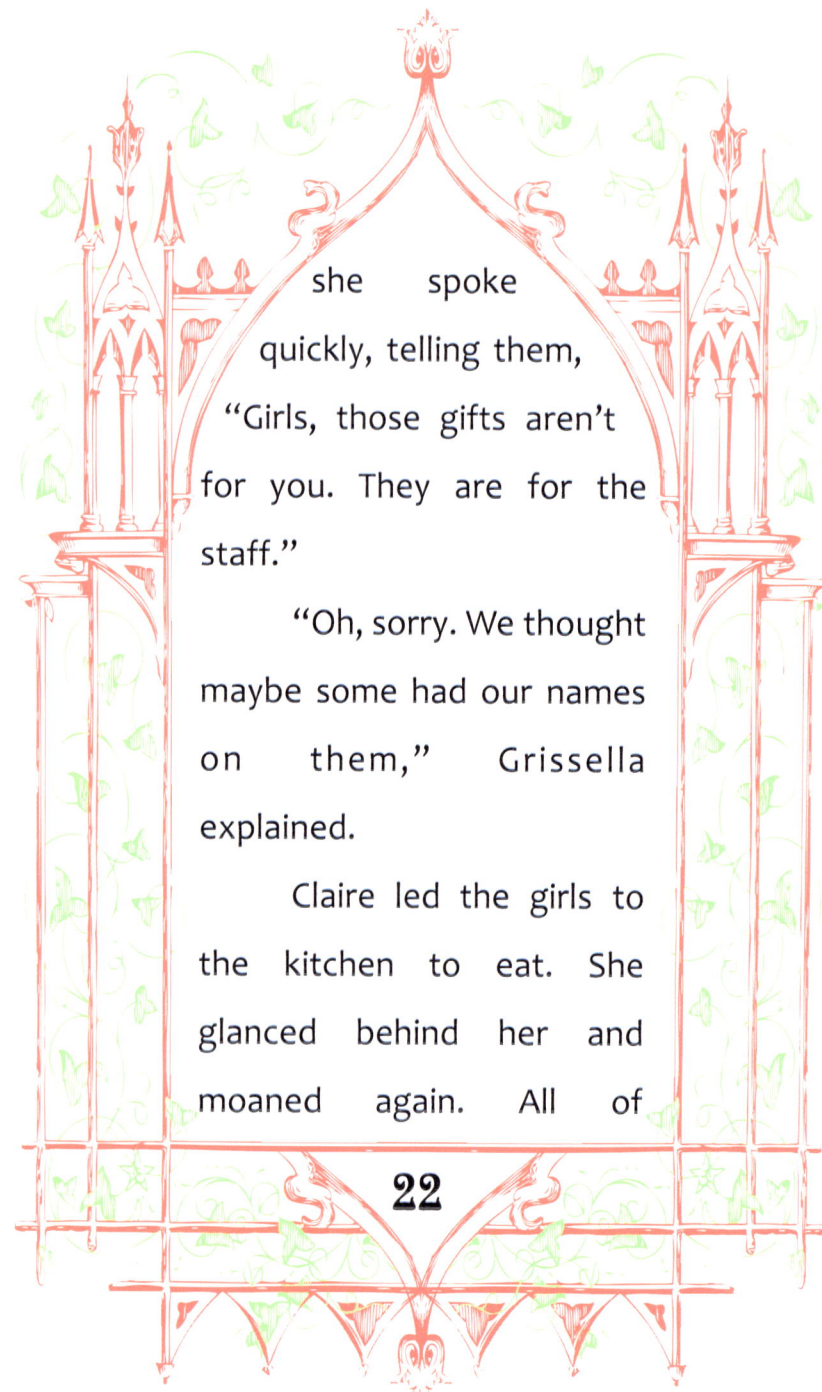

she spoke quickly, telling them, "Girls, those gifts aren't for you. They are for the staff."

"Oh, sorry. We thought maybe some had our names on them," Grissella explained.

Claire led the girls to the kitchen to eat. She glanced behind her and moaned again. All of the packages were partly torn and tossed around.

Mother came into the kitchen as the girls were finishing their breakfast. She put her hands on her hips. "What happened under the tree?" she asked loudly.

Ella spoke up quickly. "When we came down to eat, we saw Claire under the tree messing with the boxes."

Claire's eyes popped. "What?!" she exclaimed.

Her mother frowned at Claire. "What were you doing? Now all the packages will have to be rewrapped. That's a big waste of paper, ribbon and time. I'm ashamed of you, Claire. You know better than to be so destructive."

In shock, Claire stuttered, "I, I, I didn't—" But her mother's glare told her that she wasn't ready to listen. Claire bowed her head and said, "I'm sorry."

Later in the Playroom, Ella said, "I can't believe you let yourself get in trouble. Your mother was sooo mad."

Claire said, "You didn't

have to lie and say I made that mess. Why did you do that? It wasn't nice at all."

"We were curious about the boxes, but then we didn't want to get in trouble. We figured that since you are the Princess, you wouldn't be punished."

"Getting grounded or restricted or spanked isn't the only punishment, you

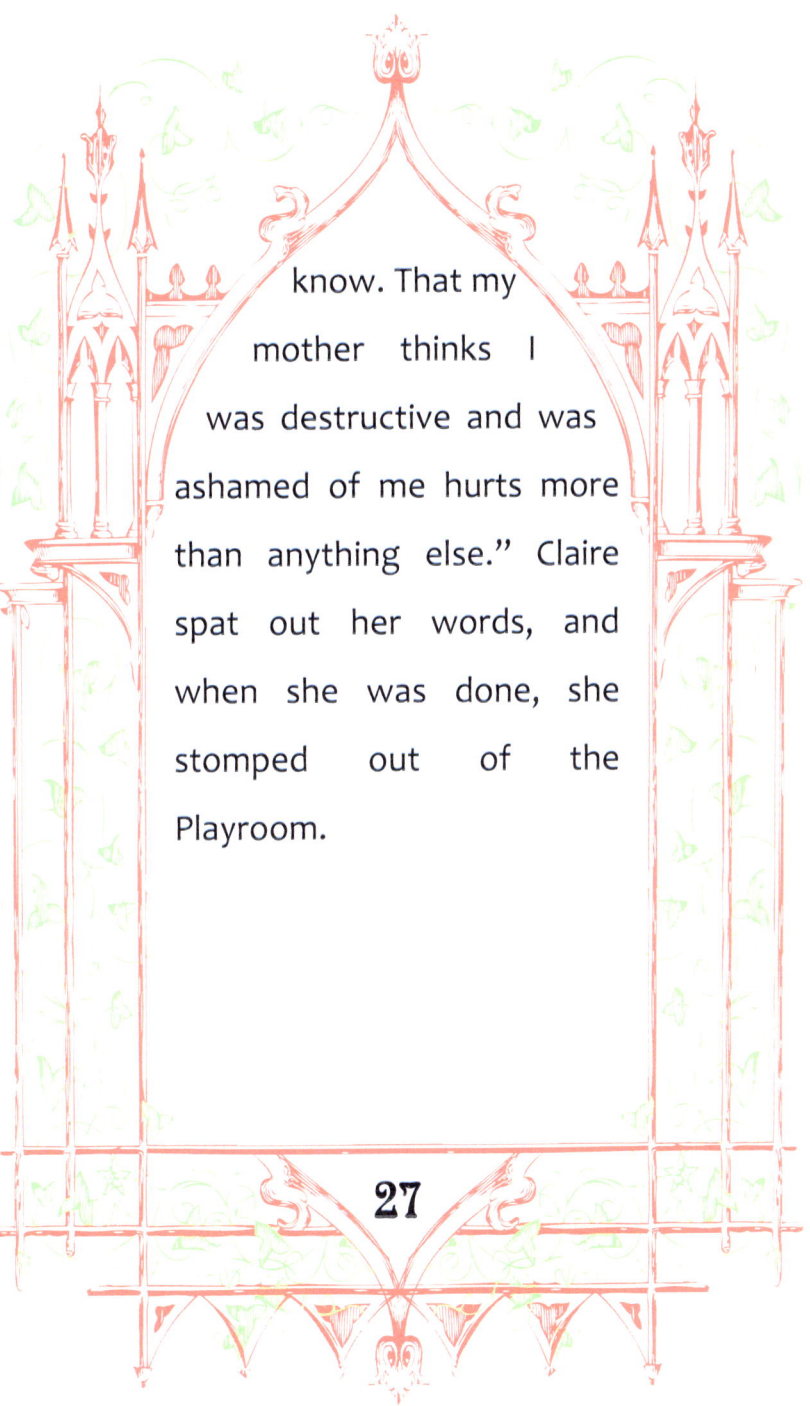

know. That my mother thinks I was destructive and was ashamed of me hurts more than anything else." Claire spat out her words, and when she was done, she stomped out of the Playroom.

Chapter Four

Princess Claire lay across her bed and cried. She didn't understand why her cousins would act so mean. If this was what Christmas was going to be like this year, she didn't want any part of it.

She fell asleep crying.

When she woke up, she crept by the Playroom and listened at the door. It was quiet, so she opened the door just a little so she could peek in. Ella and Grissella were playing quietly, not arguing at all, curious. Claire shook her head and walked on in search of her father. She found him in his office and crawled up in his lap.

"What brings you away from playing with your cousins?" he asked with a smile.

A little tear fell down Claire's cheek. "I got accused of something I didn't do, and Mother was ashamed of me. I don't know why my cousins don't like me."

The King pulled Claire

into a comforting hug. "I'm sorry, Claire."

"I just don't feel much like celebrating Christmas this year."

The King scratched his black beard as he often did when he was thinking. "Are you sure they don't like you? Did they tell you?"

"Well, not in words, but why else would they say I

made a mess of the packages under the tree when they did it? They said they didn't want to get in trouble, but it was okay if they blamed me because they thought I wouldn't be punished because I'm your daughter. And I don't understand why they tore the packages up in the first place."

"So, why would you

let your cousins disrupt your Christmas? Isn't that like getting punished twice? You can choose to let that pass. You can forgive your cousins and love them anyway. Think of the reason we celebrate Christmas. The best gift we can give is love, because we received that love from the One who created it."

Claire sat quietly for a

minute. Then she wiped her eyes. "Father, you are right as always." She smiled "Thank you." She gave her father a kiss on his cheek and hopped down off of his lap.

She went back to the Playroom, but this time there were hot words coming from inside. Ella and Grissella were arguing again. Claire thought that maybe that was the way

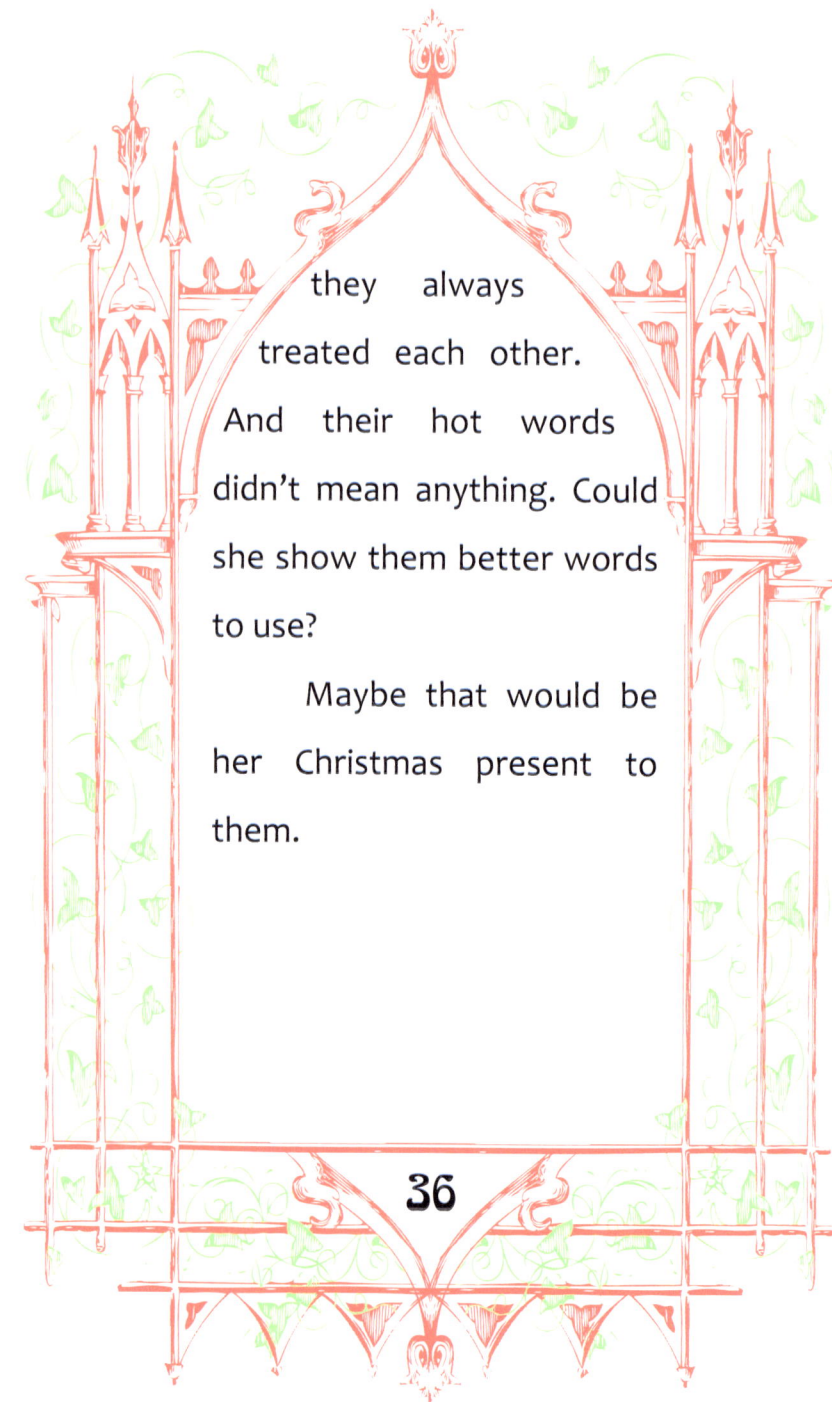

they always treated each other. And their hot words didn't mean anything. Could she show them better words to use?

Maybe that would be her Christmas present to them.

Carol Caldwell graduated from the University of Southern California with studies in English and art. She loved writing and the special magic of storytelling. Putting her stories on paper had to wait until she raised her own family, but with the arrival of grandchildren, the storyteller would not be quiet.

Carol has been formally published for a number of years and is active in writers' associations and workshops. For almost twenty years, she was a participant in a foreign exchange student program as an administrator and a host family. She has a lot of stories to tell.

Carol is a widow with two grown sons and five grandchildren, and lives in western Washington state. Her activities include being active in her church, volunteering at a women's center, and meeting with friends.

Made in the USA
Columbia, SC
27 July 2024